Gardening WITH THE EXPERTS

COTTAGE GARDENS

Gardening WITH THE EXPERTS

COTTAGE GARDENS

MARY MOODY

Bloomsbury Books
London

Front cover: A gazebo surrounded by a riot of scent and colour.

Photography: Mary Moody, David Wallace, David Young, Manuel Patty.

Published by Harlaxton Publishing Ltd
2 Avenue Road, Grantham, Lincolnshire, NG31 6TA, United Kingdom.
A Member of the Weldon International Group of Companies.

First published in 1992.

This edition published in 1993 by
Bloomsbury Books
an imprint of
The Godfrey Cave Group
42 Bloomsbury Street, London. WC1B 3QJ
under license from Harlaxton Publishing Ltd.

Publishing Manager: Robin Burgess
Project Coordinator: Mary Moody
Editor: Christine Mackinnon
Illustrator: Kathie Baxter Smith
Designed & produced for the publisher by Phillip Mathews Publishers
Produced in Singapore by Imago

British Library Cataloguing-in-Publication data.
A catalogue record for this book is available from the British Library.
Title: Gardening with the Experts: Cottage Gardens
ISBN:1 85471 107 5

CONTENTS

INTRODUCTION

Cottage garden landscaping provides the scope for creative gardeners to combine a wide range of old-fashioned flowering perennials, annuals and bulbs to create a traditional setting. Many nurseries have responded to this trend by reintroducing a wide range of long forgotten cottage garden plants. Some species have been hybridised to improve flowering, although purists will search for original stock, to give their gardens a touch of authenticity.

A cottage garden can be either a formal or an informal style, or in a larger garden, be laid out in a woodland-style. The basic design concept is to combine the varieties of fragrant climbers, roses, annuals and perennials, allowing some species to self-seed and spring anew the following season. When non-hybridised seed is available, self-seeding will happen naturally, resulting in the garden flourishing and regenerating without too much maintenance or replanting each season.

The style of the garden will depend on the way plants are combined within the landscape. Bulbs can either be interplanted with annuals and perennials, or naturalised in drifts beneath deciduous trees, or in the lawn.

Never plant bulbs in straight lines, except for low-growing edging varieties, which can most effectively frame a garden bed or the edge of a pathway.

Colour schemes

When planning a cottage garden the colour schemes can be bright and multi-coloured, or more subtle by combining pastel and cream tonings.

Terracotta edging tiles give an old-fashioned look to garden borders.

Mixed beds of annuals and perennials, including those with silver and grey foliage, are part of the cottage garden landscape.

Certain areas can be treated with mass planting of one colour, either by planting one species or a variety of species that will flower at the same time.

Bright colours — reds, yellows and purples — combine brilliantly to give a happy atmosphere to the garden. In contrast, the softer pastel shades of pink, mauve, lilac and cream are more gentle and relaxing to the eye.

Fragrance
Fragrance is a major factor in landscaping a cottage garden, since many old-fashioned species have a strong, more heady perfume than most modern hybrids.

This is particularly true of roses, which are often softer with less rigid, upright stems. Climbers should be incorporated wherever possible, to cover a fence, trellis or pergola.

Fragrant plants, whenever possible, should be planted where they can be enjoyed — next to a patio, gazebo or arbor.

Finishing touches
Old-fashioned accessories can be bought to complement this style of garden: picket fences, terracotta garden edging and borders, lattice for trellises or archways and terracotta pots will all help to create the right atmosphere.

COTTAGE GARDEN STYLES

The formal garden

Generally the design of a formal cottage garden radiates from a central path leading from the front gate to the house. Garden beds or borders of herbaceous perennials usually edge the path as well as the external fenceline and if the house has a patio, an edging bed looks most effective.

Even in small gardens a flowerbed in the centre of each side of the lawn is also popular. This can be oval, diamond or circular in shape and edged with bricks or terracotta tiles, then planted with tall species in the centre and low-growing annuals or ground-covers at the edges.

Archways covered with climbers can lead from one section of the garden to another, framing a pathway or leading from a flower garden to an area reserved for growing vegetables or herbs.

Formal gardens are, by nature, more time-consuming in terms of general maintenance. Lawns need to be fed, top-dressed and mown; edges need to be clipped and beds constantly tidied, weeded and replanted for the following season.

Above: Formal garden layout of beds and lawn, based around a central pathway to the house.
*Opposite: An archway covered with **clematis**, in full bloom.*
*Overleaf: Pathway through a grove of **azaleas mollis**, bordered by forget-me-nots.*

The woodland garden

This style of cottage garden has an untamed appearance, it requires much less upkeep than a formal garden. Woodland gardens originated in Europe, where large established deciduous trees provide a canopy for drifts of bulbs and perennials set at their base. In essence it is a garden of trees and lawn, with drifts of various bulbs emerging season by season.

To achieve an informal appearance of scattered bulbs simply throw them, by the handful, in the area where you wish them to grow, then plant them where they have fallen. Over the years they will multiply, eventually creating the desired effect of naturalised woodland.

It is important to remember that the soil around the base of trees dries out quickly in warm climates, so additional watering will be required to maintain the lawn and keep the bulbs beneath healthy .

A true woodland garden will not have formal pathways or garden beds. The emphasis is an open design without space restrictions imposed by any conventional building block. However, a woodland effect can be achieved on a small plot of land by selecting one or two appropriate large trees and a gradual establishment of naturalised plants beneath them.

The self-sown garden

This easy-care style of cottage garden depends on planting a wide range of species that seed freely and spring anew season after season. Many old-fashioned, non-hybridised plants produce seeds that scatter in the wind to produce healthy new plants, provided that the seeds land in moderately rich and moist soil. A basic framework of trees, shrubs and perennials can be planted first, then interplanted with various annuals known to seed easily.

The garden will naturally regenerate without relying on the gardener!

Choosing plants

Most nurseries stock a good range of old-fashioned plants for the cottage garden. Always select plants that are suited to your particular climate and soil, and follow planting directions carefully. The more time and energy spent preparing the ground for planting, the better the end results will be.

Try to choose a variety of plant types — annuals, perennials and bulbs — that will flower over many months, to keep the garden in constant colour. Consider colour combinations, avoid clashing schemes, and set aside at least one area for a massed planting or colour theme garden.

A woodland garden where plants are allowed to run wild and self-seed.

GENERAL MAINTENANCE

Even a low maintenance woodland cottage garden will need a degree of care and attention if plants are to thrive in their environment. Garden maintenance need not be a tedious chore if some organisation is applied. Set aside some time each week for general maintenance tasks such as mulching, weeding, watering and feeding, and the results will speak for themselves.

Mulching

A well-mulched garden seems to thrive no matter how harsh the climate or how poor the original soil. An alterative to mulching is to use inorganic materials such as plastic (black plastic is quite popular) but this has a tendency to smother the soil and reduce air flow. Organic mulches, on the other hand, greatly improve soil texture as well as providing many other benefits.

Mulching is beneficial for various reasons. It stops weeds emerging from the soil around the base of plants and between rows. It keeps the soil moist between waterings, prevents the surface from drying out and improves soil texture by keeping it lightly moist. If organic mulch is used a steady stream of nutrients is supplied to plant roots. As the mulch layer breaks down the mulch builds the soil into rich, friable humus.

The ideal time to mulch is when young plants are established, or immediately after planting. Take care not to mulch too close to the base of the seedlings. A good deep mulch is the best. There are layers of mulch that serve different purposes, for example, a layer of blood and bone at ground level to provide immediate nutrients, a layer of well-rotted manure to keep the soil moist and gradually break down, improving texture or a top layer of pine bark to prevent the manure from either drying out or blowing away. The most effective mulch is a thick one, to a depth of about 8-10cm (3-4in). Never bring the mulch layer in contact with the base of trees or shrubs above the planting line, or

A thick layer of organic mulch will help to keep weed growth down, while providing nutrients.

*A sloping bed of **Chamomile** and **Achillea**, edged with logs
to prevent mulch from washing away.*

too close to the stems of young seedlings, as
this can create an excess of moisture and
lead to fungal problems.

Weeding
Although considered a tedious chore,
weeding is essential to prevent plants from
being swamped and overgrown by un-
wanted species. There are alternatives to
spending hours on your hands and knees
doing battle with weeds in garden beds.

Weeding damp soil is much, easier than
trying to weed dry ground. If beds require a
clean out, always water well the day before
to ensure the weeds lift out easily without
disturbing the roots of shrubs, annuals,
bulbs and perennials. As weeds compete for

moisture and nutrients, plants in an
overgrown garden will not be as healthy
and robust as those allowed to grow and
develop in a carefully tended weed-free
environment.

When plants are weakened by this
competition they become susceptible to
attack and infestation by all sorts of pests,
insects and diseases.

In an old-fashioned garden there are all
sorts of weeds — such as dandelions and
clover — that look quite pretty in small
clumps scattered through beds of perennials, but take care that they do not take a
stranglehold, multiplying and overriding
other species.

Weeds are generally species that are so

tough and hardy that they will survive in almost any conditions. They also self-sow and multiply quickly, invading all parts of your own garden, as well as your neighbours'. To prevent weed growth use preventive measures like mulching the ground well around new plants, and removing existing weeds before they have a chance to produce flowers and propagate.

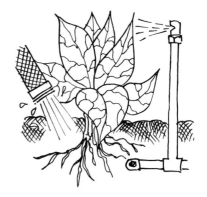

Watering

The amount of water required by your garden depends on many factors, such as the type of soil in the garden. Light, sandy soils dry out quickly and therefore require more watering. Heavy clay soils hold the moisture longer but don't necessarily allow it to reach plant roots effectively. Both soil types will improve if organic matter is added to help its texture and water holding capacity. The garden design will also

Regular watering is required during hot and dry summer weather.

influence how much water is required. A garden of flowering shrubs and annuals will certainly require more attention than a garden of established trees and hardy

*Charming **Bellis perennis** used as a border, backed by **camellias** and **rhododendrons**.*

15

Watering by hand helps maintain a close watch on plants, checking for pests or diseases.

Dry fertiliser applied as a side-dressing on moist soil that has been lightly turned over.

shrubs. Lawns are also fairly demanding, especially during high summer when, without enough water, they will tend to wither or fade.

The best way to reduce watering is to mulch the soil surface beneath spreading trees, shrubs and on garden beds. Mulching acts as a protective layer between the soil and the elements, helping to reduce drying out and surface caking. Avoid creating garden beds at the base of trees that are going to grow very large, as the tree roots will compete for moisture with whatever is planted in those beds. Take advantage of the partial shade created by the ends of the branches rather than the total shade near the base of the trunk!

Consider incorporating hedges and windbreaks into the landscape. By reducing the effect of the prevailing winds and providing a warm, sheltered environment, you will create a micro-climate that is suited to the cultivation of many species that will require less watering.

During high summer it is advisable to water early in the morning or, better still early evening — simply wait until the direct sun has moved from the garden before getting the sprinklers going. In winter, in cold climates, if watering is necessary, do so mid-morning rather than late afternoon to avoid frost damage.

Feeding

Many cottage garden perennials and annuals are heavy feeders and demand good rich soil conditions to produce lush foliage and an abundance of flowers.

The soil should be enriched prior to planting with plenty of organic matter — composts or manures — then regularly mulched to keep up the supply of nutrients.

Some plants benefit from a boost of liquid plant food when buds are forming, mix a liquid fertiliser with water and apply direct to the ground with a watering can.

Dry plant food can be applied as a side dressing, lightly dug into the soil surface around those plants that need a boost.

Overleaf: A terracotta dovecote elevated safely from the reach of predators such as cats.

OLD-FASHIONED
PERENNIALS

In gardening terms, perennial refers to a wide group of evergreen and herbaceous plants that have a flowering life of three years or more. Perennials differ from shrubs which have more woody stems and a more permanent place in the garden.

Cottage gardens traditionally are filled with a range of perennial plants, providing a solid background for the planting of bulbs, annuals and ground covers. Most perennials will die back in winter and reappear in spring for many seasons. They can be easily propagated by lifting and dividing the clumps in autumn.

Useful perennials

Acanthus mollis (oyster plant): valued for its foliage as well as flowers, *Acanthus* has large dark and glossy leaves and tall flower spikes covered in papery white and beige flowers.

Achillea (yarrow): various species, many with attractive silvery grey foliage and flowers that vary from golden yellow to rose pink.

Aconitum (monkshood): dark green, glossy foliage and deep blue or purple-blue hooded flowers borne in racemes.

Agapanthus: an easy-to-grow old-fashioned favourite, with glossy green strap-like leaves, while the blooms are a spectacular circular ball of either white or mauve-blue flowers.

Alchemilla (lady's mantle): this perennial forms a clump of grey-green foliage and masses of lemon-green flowers.

Ajuga reptans (bugle flower): a hardy groundcover with foliage of deep bronzy green, or variegated cream and light green, and short spikes of blue-purple flowers.

Alstroemeria aurantiaca: fleshy foliage and trumpet-shaped flowers of orange, yellow, mauve-pink or purple, spotted with brown.

Androsace (rock jasmine): pretty flowers

Tall varieties need to be supported with stakes as they grow and come into flower.

The huge crêpe flowers of the **paeony**.

that resemble phlox and are either crimson or pink with yellow centres; prefers cool to cold climate.

Anemone (woodland anemone): a low-growing plant with soft green foliage and single blue flowers in spring; also white, pink and violet forms available.

Anthemis nobilis (chamomile): delicate light green foliage and small white daisies with yellow centres; quite a few different species in this group, all with pretty daisy flowers.

Aquilegia (columbine): the perennial form has delicate green foliage and most attractive flowers that are either plain colours, or two-tone in the apricot, pink, cream, maroon and purple colour range.

Arctotis (aurora daisy): pretty daisies with masses of mauve, purple and deep red flowers and grey-green foliage.

Armeria (thrift): a tufted plant with grey-green foliage and circular flowerheads of papery blooms that are pink, white or red in colour.

Artemesia absinthium (wormwood): an aromatic plant valued for its attractive lacy grey foliage.

Aster novi-belgii (michaelmas daisy): a group of flowering plants with both dwarf and full size varieties and sprays of delicate daisy flowers that vary from white through purple, lavender, blue, pink and mauve.

Astilbe (goat's beard): handsome foliage and delicate sprays of tiny flowers in the mauve, pink, white and red colour range.

Bergenia cordifolia (Norwegian snow): leathery foliage and small stems of pink

Chrysanthemums have many flower forms, most of them large and showy.

flowers in winter and early spring.
Campanula medium (Canterbury bells): various forms of hardy perennial, some are valuable groundcovers, while others are effective in a herbaceous border.
Chrysanthemum frutescens (marguerite daisy): a group of showy plants with large daisy flowers; may require staking for support.
Chrysanthemum maximum (shasta daisy): hardy and free flowering white daisies with yellow centres; excellent cut flowers with long stems.
Delphinium: an old-fashioned perennial which is classified as an annual in warm regions, however it will pop up for several years in a row in cool to cold climates.
Dicentra spectabilis (bleeding heart): a low-growing plant with heart-shaped red

flowers on arching stems; the greyish foliage is fern-like and most attractive.
Digitalis (foxgloves): ideal for a massed planting, the tall slender flower stalks of foxgloves give a spectacular display with blooms that are cream, mauve, pink and purple with deeper tonings in the centre.
Dimorphotheca (black-eyed Susan): deep green foliage and white daisy flowers with deep blue centres.
Erigeron macranthus: the foliage is delicate and feathery while the small daisy flowers are mauve with yellow centres.
Gaillardia (blanket flower): clumps of greyish foliage with striking silky maroon flowers edged in golden yellow; likes good soil and drainage and an open, sunny position.
Gazania: good for dry climates, with brilliant coloured daisy flowers with contrasting centres.
Geranium (crane's bill): fleshy foliage and small, fragrant flowers; many varieties that should be pruned to maintain bushy growth.
Gerbera jamesonii (African daisy): a small clump of slender leaves and a tall stalk topped by a showy flower that can be red, yellow, orange, pink or white. Require mild climate.
Geum: a spreading perennial with yellow or red/orange poppy flowers; also a dwarf form available.
Gypsophila paniculata (gypsophila): the perennial form has an abundance of delicate white or pink flowers; prefers moderate to cool climates and soil to which some lime has been added.
Helleborus orientalis (Christmas rose): good for shady places, it has deep green foliage and exquisite pendant flowers that are

*Opposite: A delightful stream and pond edged with old-fashioned plants, **Stachys** and **Erigeron**.*

*A formal garden with **magnolias** in bloom, **polyanthus** and **primulas** in the foreground.*

cream flushed with mauve.

Houstonia: small clumps of delicate leaves and masses of tiny blue flowers on slender stem; plant in semi-shade in deep, moist soil.

Iberis sempervirens (perennial candytuft): forms a dense mass of deep green foliage covered with circular white flowerheads.

Liatris spicata (gay feather): a compact plant with slender leaves and spikes of pink/purple flowers during spring.

Limonium sinuatum (statice): papery flowers in the blue/purple colour range.

Lupinus (Russell lupins): the perennial form of lupin forms a low clump of foliage and tall spikes of brilliant flowers in most shades of the spectrum; makes a spectacular massed planting.

Lychnis coronaria (rose campion): white woolly foliage and slender stems of white or crimson flowers in summer and autumn.

Paeonia (paeony): a group of flowering perennials with attractive foliage with huge crepe flowers, sometimes as large as a dinner plate!

Papaver orientale (oriental poppy): tall stems of greyish foliage and huge saucer-shaped blooms of red, scarlet, pink, white or mauve.

Phlox paniculata (perennial phlox): during spring the foliage emerges, followed by stems of purple flowers that can reach 1 metre (3ft) in height.

Platycodon (balloon flower): slender stems with delicate balloon shaped bulbs that open to star-like blue flowers; very pretty; also a white form available.

Rudbeckia laciniata (golden glow): tall stems topped by brilliant yellow flowers during late summer and autumn; this group includes *Rudbeckia hybrida* which is grown as an annual.

Stachys lantana (lamb's ear): spreading clumps of velvety grey foliage and tall mauve flower spikes. For mild regions.

Teucrium chamaedrys (wall germander): low-growing perennial with lilac-rose, white-lipped flowers in spring.

Trollius (globe flowers): a spring-flowering perennial with brilliant orange or yellow flowers according to the species. Thrives in moist areas.

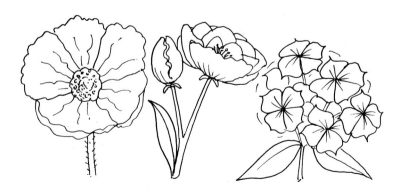

Papaver orientale *(oriental poppy),* **Paeony** *and* **Phlox***.*

Stachys lantana *(lamb's ear) has soft velvety grey foliage*
followed by tall mauve flower spikes.

Verbena x *hybrida* (verbena): flowers of red, white, pink or lavender; grows to 40cm (15in) in height; blooms during summer.

Veronica incana (veronica): excellent border or rockery plant with grey-green foliage and pretty blue flowers; foliage forms a ground covering matt.

Viola odorata (sweet violet): Clumps of deep green foliage with delicate flowers that range in colour from white through shades of mauve to deep purple; strong fragrant flowers.

FRAGRANT FLOWERS

Fragrance is an important aspect of old-fashioned gardening as so many of the original non-hybrid flower forms had very strong aromas.

A carefully planned cottage garden will always include a range of fragrant plants located where they can be walked upon thus releasing the scent or simply enjoyed in comfortable surroundings. Ideally they should be planted adjacent to verandahs, patios, pergolas or a summer house, so their beauty can be appreciated.

Fragrant roses can be trained over an archway leading from one area of the garden to another.

Some care must be taken in the placement of fragrant plants so that they do not overpower or clash with each other. Often species have a delicate or subtle scent which can be lost or distorted if placed too near another strongly fragrant plant.

Rosemary and lavender are good examples of species that blend well together. Even though they both have quite distinctive individual fragrances, they complement each other and are often grouped throughout a cottage garden landscape.

The fragrant lawn
Try an alternative to conventional lawn by planting fragrant groundcovers which work well in certain situations.

There are various suitable species which eliminate the need for mowing while providing a delightful aroma when walked upon. Chamomile (*Anthemis nobilis*), thyme (*Thymus vulgaris*) and pennyroyal (*Mentha pulegium*) are good choices, while strawberry clover (*Trifolium fragiferum*) has also been used successfully in a wide range of soils and climates.

Trees
Some trees, suited to warmer regions, are valued for their fragrant flowers and/or foliage. Lemon-scented myrtle (*Backhousia citriodora*) and lemon-scented gum (*Eucalyptus citriodora*) both exude a heady citrus

fragrance, while the deciduous magnolia tree is known the world over for its exotic spring display of fragrant flowers.

Trees worth planting for aroma are camphor laurel (*Cinnamomum camphora*) which has camphor-scented leaves; and frangipani (*Hymenosporum flavum*) which has richly scented yellow flowers in spring and summer.

Black locust tree (*Robinia pseudoacacia*) with white pea-like flowers, is suited to cooler regional climates.

Shrubs

There are many fragrant shrubs to choose from, including lavender (*Lavandula* species), daphne (*Daphne odora*) and rosemary (*Rosmarinus officinalis*). These are known and loved by all but consider also less commonly cultivated species like *Brunfelsia calycina* with fragrant violet-blue flowers which fade through lavender to white. It is suited to greenhouse cultivation in cooler regions. This fading effect is also found in *Robinia pseudoacacia*, common name black locust tree, with white pea-like flowers; yesterday, today and tomorrow.

Other worthwhile fragrant shrubs include: Lemon verbena (*Aloysia triphylla*) with light green scented foliage; brown boronia (*Boronia megastigma*), with gold and brown scented flowers in winter; lilac (*Buddleia davidii*) with panicles of lilac flowers in summer; Mexican orange blossom (*Choisya ternata*) with pure white scented blooms; common lilac (*Syringa vulgaris*) whose flowers may be pink, deep purple, lilac or white; and *Viburnum* x *burkwoodii*, prized for its fragrant waxy white flowers.

Old-fashioned roses are generally very fragrant, and resistant to pests and diseases.

Bulbs

Lily of the valley (*Convallaria majalis*), Freesias; grape hyacinth (*Muscari*), daffodils and jonquils (*Narcissus*), plantain lily (*Hosta plantaginea*) and day lily (*Hemerocallis*)

Perennials

Garden Phlox, Violets and cottage Pinks are the most favoured, while annuals, too, bring colour as well as fragrance.

Annuals

Pansies, nasturtiums, sweet peas, larkspurs, stocks, wallflowers, snapdragons and sweet Alice are all delightfully fragrant.

Overleaf: **Syringia vulgaris** (*common lilac*) *produces panicles of purple, lilac or white fragrant flowers in spring.*

29

The most satisfying time to enjoy the fragrance of various plants will vary according to the species. Some emerge as the sun brings warmth to the day, while others wait and linger in the late afternoon.

Incorporate aromatic plants around a gazebo, where their fragrance can be enjoyed.

COTTAGE GARDEN ROSES

Renewed interest in old-fashioned plant varieties has extended into the world of roses, where long-forgotten favourites are now being bred and sold to an eager market.

There are various reasons for this renewed interest in cottage garden roses. They suit the style and design of old-fashioned gardens, especially bush and rambling roses with their soft outlines and bowers of blooms. Most of these old varieties require less fuss and attention than their modern counterparts.

It is true to say that most of the original varieties are less prone to pests and diseases, once established, they will survive happily for many years without much care or attention. They do not require routine pruning and shaping, and should be allowed to grow naturally with only the dead wood and spent flowers trimmed back from time to time.

Care of roses

To grow roses successfully, first work to create the ideal growing conditions. Roses that are planted in moderately rich and well-drained soil will be stronger and more resistant to pests and diseases.

Mulching well also helps to keep the soil temperature more even, cuts down on weeds and prevents the ground from drying out in hot weather.

To create a good growing environment, start six months ahead of planting time. The soil should be friable to a depth of 50cm (20in) and be free of weeds — you can mulch with newspaper to suppress weed growth, or slash weeds and cover the soil surface with a thick mulch of compost, well-rotted manures or grass clippings (leaf mould is also excellent). To correct any soil acidity sprinkle the soil surface with dolomite, blood and bone, or wood ashes.

Noisette climbers are valued for their prolific flowers and delightful fragrance.

Overleaf: Cottage garden roses, such as **rugosa** 'Alba' often have simple, open flowers with prominent stamens.

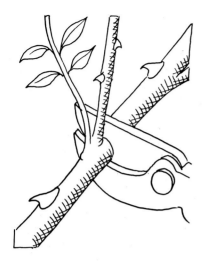

Remove dead or diseased wood from roses using clean, sharp secateurs.

Plant roses as soon a possible after purchase, making sure that the soil is lightly damp (as well as the potting mix around the roses) prior to planting. Allow sufficient distance between plants — this will vary according to the variety. Take care when planting climbing varieties not to position them under eaves as the soil will be too dry for their liking. Do provide good support and encourage the climbing stems to cover a trellis or pergola by tying them up gently. Once established, roses should be mulched regularly with a well-rotted compost or manure, and watered frequently although never overwatered as this will cause fungal diseases.

Although it is possible to plant between roses with annuals or small perennials, keep in mind that these will compete with the roses for nutrients and moisture, and may create moist ground conditions which can result in fungal disease. Roses require plenty of 'breathing' space at ground level, and overplanting will restrict air circulation around plants.

Let this sit for six months without disturbance, except to remove the odd weed that appears, the ground will then be well-prepared for planting.

POT POURRI

Collect the petals of fragrant flowers and use them to make a sweet-smelling pot pourri.
This traditional method produces a delicate and warmly-fragrant mix that can be made in quantity
and used throughout the house.

2 CUPS ROSE PETALS
3 CUPS CARNATION PETALS
1/2 CUP ORRIS ROOT POWDER
1 TABLESPOON CINNAMON
12 CLOVES
4 DROPS OF ROSE OIL

Dry the flower petals separately, then combine them and sprinkle on the orris powder.
Mix in the rose oil, cinnamon and cloves and mix well by hand (the warmth helps to bring
out the fragrance.) Keep covered for at least a month before using.

Most old varieties do not require regular pruning or spraying like their modern counterparts.

Disease resistant varieties:
Rosa rugosa: very hardy, even in difficult soils and climates.
Recommended varieties are: 'Delicata' which has fragrant lilac-pink double flowers; 'Belle Poidevine' which has large double pink/mauve blooms; 'Calacarpo' which has single lilac pink flowers and red rosehips; 'Carmenetta' which has small pink flowers and bronze foliage; 'Fimbriata' which is a double white with frilled petals flowering over many months; 'Micrugosa' has a dense, bushy shape and light pink single flowers; 'Pink Guttendorst' has pretty fringed pink flowers, reminiscent of carnations; 'Scabrosa' which has large, showy, single purple flowers with yellow stamens; all very fragrant and a joy to grow.
Rugosa 'Alba': marvellous for recurrent flowers; large white showy blooms and red rosehips.
Rugosa rubra: pretty single flowers in the purple/red colour range. A very prolific bloomer.

Wild roses and wild climbers:
Gallica: also known as French roses, which are hardy with fragrant double blooms.
Damask roses: very old and beautiful varieties, dating back to Egyptian times.

Alba roses: soft and fragrant blooms of pink, cream, white or blush.

Portland roses: small, compact bushes with large double flowers.

Centifolia roses: also known as cabbage roses. Lovely double fragrant flowers.

China roses: good for small gardens, bloom into winter.

Bourbon roses: a cross between China and Bourbon roses. Large, sweetly scented flowers. Prolific flowering.

Tea roses: vigorous bushes, elegant and delicately coloured blooms. A favourite in cottage gardens.

Noisette roses: vigorous climbing roses, delightful fragrant blooms.

Donkey roses: old-fashioned miniature roses, very tiny flowers.

Ramblers: ideal for training over archways, trellises or doorways. Graceful shape, fragrant flowers.

Most rose nurseries and specialist rose shops have a section devoted to old-fashioned or cottage garden varieties. Ask the advice of the nursery owner and select a variety of plants for different purposes. Perhaps bush roses for a grouped display, also ramblers or climbers to cover a trellis or unsightly fence.

A walled garden creates a microclimate, protected from strong winds.

ANNUALS

There are certainly plenty of pretty annuals that are ideal for planting in a cottage garden landscape.

By definition, annuals are those plants whose life cycle is completed within a twelve month period. Annuals are grown from seed which germinates, flowers and 'goes to seed' before dying. The actual growing period for annuals varies considerably from species to species — some will produce flowers only eight weeks from the sowing of the seeds, while biennials take two full seasons to mature and flower. In general, annuals are either sown in autumn for early spring flowering, or sown in spring for summer flowering.

Self-seeding

Many annuals will self-seed and spring again season after season, giving the garden a naturally 'wild' appearance. Look for non-hybridised seeds to achieve this effect. Ensure that the soil is rich and moist for the best results.

The secret of self-seeding is to allow some of the flowers to remain untouched until they have completely withered and died back. The seed will be released from pods as the plant dies back, and these should be allowed to blow in the wind or fall wherever they choose. Do not cultivate the ground at all, except perhaps to pull out those weeds which seem to be taking over (after a few years the annuals will swamp the weeds, with luck!).

If the weather is dry, water the ground well, as this is vital for germination.

Annuals for the cottage garden

Ageratum (floss flower): masses of fluffy lavender blue flowers and mid-green foliage.
Alyssum (sweet Alice): very easy to grow, *Alyssum* covers the ground with a carpet of colour — white, mauve-pink or lavender.

Annuals can be grown from seedlings transplanted when large enough to handle.

*Delightful **Alyssum** forms a carpet and flowers for many months during summer and autumn.*

Amaranthus: various forms of this attractive plant exist, with flowers in the bronze, red and yellow colour range.

Antirrhinum (snapdragon): varies in height according to variety; the best displays are of mixed colour, ranging from white tinged with yellow through every shade of yellow, orange, pink and mauve to darkest red.

Bellis perennis (English daisy): these delightful plants will come back season after season, especially in cool climates, as the botanical name 'perennis' suggests. English daisies are pretty, with circular daisy flowers in every shade from white through mauve, pink and maroon.

Calendula (English marigold): showy flowers in the yellow-orange colour range, carried on short stems.

Callistephus chinensis (aster): excellent cut flowers, asters have long stems and large, showy flowers with quilled petals.

Celosia argentea 'Cristata' (cockscomb): feathery flowers of bronze, red, orange and yellow; there are dwarf forms, growing to about 35cm (14in), and a taller form that reaches 75cm (30in) to make an excellent fill-in or background plant.

Centaurea cyanus (cornflower): Bright blue or pink button flowers in profusion during late spring and summer.

Cheiranthus cheiri (wallflower): forms a carpet of fragrant golden flowers; also purple and creamy varieties available.

Cineraria: a low to medium-growing annual that produces showy clumps of flowers of pale pink, mauve, purple or maroon.

Coreopsis (*Calliopsis*): an annual that easily self-sows, with clumps of bright green foliage and brilliant yellow daisy flowers; also mauve/lilac forms.

Cosmos: excellent background plant, growing to 2 metres (6ft) in height with pale pink, mauve and purple flowers. There are also some smaller growing varieties in the gold and yellow colour range.

Delphinium ajacis (larkspur): Tall spikes for the back of the garden, with bright blue or mauve-blue flowers.

Dianthus (carnations, pinks): The larger species (carnations) are one of the most popular cut flowers, while the smaller versions (pinks) are excellent cottage garden specimens. Both are quite easy to grow as a bedding annual, providing the soil is moderately rich and limy.

Eschscholzia californica (California poppy): poppy flowers that are easy and fast to grow, with lacy foliage, soft, open flowers.

Many varieties can also be raised from seeds sown directly where the plant is to grow.

Gypsophila elegans (baby's breath): delicate, feathery plants with lacy bright green foliage, masses of tiny snow white flowers.

Impatiens (balsam): easy to grow; flowers are small but bright and showy, single or double forms; colours ranging from white through to dark red.

Lathyrus (sweet pea): exquisite climbing annuals have masses of delicate flowers in various shades of red, pink, purple and white; dwarf forms also available.

Linaria cymbalaria (toadflax): tiny flowers that are similar to snapdragons, in cream, mauve, purple and bronze; sow seeds in autumn for spring flowering.

Lobelia : edging plant with a cascading habit; green/bronze foliage and masses of tiny bright blue flowers in spring, summer and autumn.

Lunaria annua (honesty): tall, slender annual with purple-mauve flowers and unusual transluscent seed pods which can be dried for indoor arrangements.

Malcolmia maritima (virginian stocks): spikes of glorious perfumed flowers in colours ranging from white through every shade of pink and mauve to deep purple and rose.

Mesembryanthemum (Livingstone daisy): bright, colourful daisy flowers for an open, sunny position; flowers open only when the sun is on them.

Myosotis sylvatica (forget-me-nots): tiny bright blue flowers and mid-green foliage; plants will self-sow and spring up all over the garden if allowed.

Nemophila menziesii (baby blue eyes): ground covering annual that forms a carpet of pleasant green foliage and bright blue flowers with white centres.

Nigella (love-in-a-mist): soft, feathery foliage and a mass of bright blue flowers with black centres.

*Colourful **Nasturtiums** cascade over rocks — here a form with variegated foliage.*

Papaver (poppy): brilliant flowers in a wide range of warm colours. Poppies are generally sown from seed or seedling during late summer and autumn, for flowering in midwinter right through spring.

Petunia: fast-growing and colourful, with many flower forms and varieties.

Portulaca: a colourful succulent that covers the ground with green foliage and masses of bright flowers that open in the sun; position in an open, sunny location and water well.

Primula: both annual and perennial forms of primula (the variety *Primula malacoïdes* is the annual) with ground covering foliage

***Tagetes** (marigolds) can be used to repel insects from the herb or vegetable garden.*

*Overleaf: The bright open faces of **violas**, available in many varieties including some that will self-sow.*

43

and tall slender spikes of delicate flowers through various shades of pink and mauve.

Rudbeckia hirta 'Tetra' (gloriosa daisy): medium to tall-growing annual with soft daisy flowers of orange, bronze and yellow with black centres.

Statice now Limonium (sea lavender): papery flowers on stiff stems — purple, yellow, blue, pink or white; excellent as a dried flower, holds colour well.

Tagetes (marigold): brilliant flowers in the orange, yellow, russet and red colour range; marigolds are a useful border plant, especially in vegetable and herb gardens where they help to repel insects.

Tropaeolum majus (nasturtium): good for poorer soil; has a trailing habit, circular foliage and colourful red, orange or yellow flowers.

Viola (pansy): attractive foliage and glorious open-faced flowers in a wide range of colours from almost black to white, and every imaginable colour combination in between.

Zinnia: dazzling display of bright flowers that are red, orange, yellow pink and purple; hardy and easy to grow, especially in warm climates.

INDEX